Getting Rid of Stage Fright

A Little Book of Horrors and How to Deal with Them

Book 2

Andrea Strunz

Contents

Acknowledgment

As always, I want to give thanks where it is due.
First Hope Kouri, my wonderful graphic designer, who comes along for the ride enthusiastically every time. I wouldn't know what to do without you. You make my writing life so much easier.

This book wouldn't have happened without my hypnotherapy and NLP teachers. And not only the big names, who are awesome anyway, but also all the trainers, who were patient, talked a lot about their experiences, and helped me whenever I had questions. Thank you for sharing your wisdom.

Also, a big thank you to my hypnotherapy colleague Diane Baxter and to Amanda Chow for proofreading and editing. Your input is valuable and all mistakes are mine.

Thank you to everyone else, you know who you are.

"ACCORDING TO MOST STUDIES, PEOPLE'S NUMBER ONE FEAR IS PUBLIC SPEAKING. NUMBER TWO IS DEATH. DEATH IS NUMBER TWO. DOES THAT SOUND RIGHT? THIS MEANS TO THE AVERAGE PERSON, IF YOU GO TO A FUNERAL, YOU'RE BETTER OFF IN THE CASKET THAN DOING THE EULOGY." - Jerry Seinfield

Chapter 1

About you

For whom this book is for.

If you've decided to read a book about getting rid of stage fright, you are probably in the group of readers for whom I have written this. But just to make sure, here is who I had in mind.

This is for you

- If you are an artist or entertainer who needs or wants to go on stage on a regular basis but every time you come near a stage, you freeze and feel sick. Your brain is an empty hole, and you can't remember a word you wanted to say.
And you are sure, that as soon as you can tear your glued-on feet from the floor and take one step forward you will fall on your nose with all five or five thousand people in the audience laughing their heads off.
And no, it is not part of your comedy routine.

- If you are a musician and you feel like you are back in your first music class ever probably when you were four years old. What is this thing, how do I hold it and how the heck do I get some music out of it? Your sweating hands do not help a bit.

- If you are a singer who croaks worse than a frog with a cold whenever he/she sees a microphone standing in the middle of a stage, where you feel all alone and lost while your audience is staring at you, just waiting to tear you apart. And I am not even speaking about the critics that must be around somewhere.

- If you are an actor, maybe with or without acting training and you dream of being on stage but those lights will kill you. And your brain feels like Swiss cheese.

- If you are still very young, either a child or a teenager, being shy and doubting yourself a lot and you have to sing, dance or perform otherwise in front of people, them being family or strangers.

- If you know someone who has a problem with stage fright, maybe you are teaching someone who needs to go on stage, and you want to help. Read this and give the techniques to other people with my blessings.

This is not or not exactly for you.

- If you need to hold a presentation either at work or in school. Yes, you can use all those techniques in the book. They will work just fine and are also for you.
  But then, please don't mind that my examples and stories will be all around the entertainment business.

- If you are looking for how to make your presentation content better. There are other books out there that concentrate on content and how to get into rapport with your audience. In this book, we are only dealing with the mental issue of stage fright. This excruciating fear either makes you roll into the embryo position and cry or sends you into the deer in headlights mode.

You are still with me? Great. Then let's move on. I bet you have a lot of questions about this book, and about me and are curious why my techniques are better than the 486 others you have tried before.

> "I cannot do all the good that the world needs. But the world needs all the good that I can do."
> — Jana Stanfield

Chapter 2

About me

Who am I and why should you listen to me?
Just to make it clear, you are an adult, and you don't have to listen to me at all. You make your own decisions but just in case I do know more than you about this topic, what do you have to lose?
And if you are not an adult yet, see me as a nice benevolent teacher or your nice crazy aunt who really wants to help you live the best and most pain-free life you can have. I want you to rock your life and not life rock you.

Let me start with a short bio of myself. My professional life started out after university as a social worker and a short time later becoming a teacher for adults (and still doing the same social work just not getting paid for it).
I was teaching German as a foreign language.
In both professions I met many people with mental health issues, some of them severe.
And even though I wanted to help, I sadly lacked the knowledge.

Shortly before Covid, I started training as a hypnotherapist having stumbled upon one of my teachers on the internet, trying her audio hypnosis on me and having amazing results.
And I haven't stopped learning since as the topic fascinates me.
I had the great honor and opportunity to be trained by some of the best and most famous hypnotherapists and RTT therapists in the world with their excellent training staff, some of them being extraordinary hypnotherapists and coaches themselves. Also throw in some NLP just for good measure.
They were all very generous in teaching their knowledge and giving forth their wisdom accumulated in many years of practice, helping me get a better understanding of how the mind works and how to help with psychological issues of many different kinds. So, my professional background is solid.

Why should you listen to me in regard to stage fright? I do know my way around a stage, maybe not the one you are on, but something similar.

In my early childhood, I suffered some situations around performing, which should have prevented me from getting on a stage ever again, but thankfully it didn't. Let me tell you about my story.

Like many children, I was part of family events like Christmas and birthday parties, where everyone sang, either in a group or solo. And being the oldest child, I had to at least in the beginning.
Why only in the beginning, because very soon everyone told me not to sing, as I couldn't hit a note if my life depended on it. Still can't by the way. Except under a shower, then I sing great.
So, after being excluded from singing at family events, knowing I couldn't sing, school started. And with-it music lessons. Guess what we had to do? Yes, singing. Alone in front of the whole class. During elementary school, there must have been a consent not to give bad marks but I wasn't allowed to join our school choir, which hurt.

Later in Gymnasium (for all English native speakers, no, that is not a sports thing, it is the highest form of secondary education, aiming to prepare students for continued university education) I still had to stand in front of my class and sing. This time I got marks and I got my first 6, which is the worst mark you can get in Germany. If you have one in your year's end report, you have to repeat the whole year. Thankfully I was good in music theory, so I could smooth it over. Still, standing there, I was shaking like a leftover leaf in a winter storm.

As my parents wanted to give me a broad education, they sent me to music school in the afternoons, where I first learned how to play the flute and later piano.
Learning instruments wasn't the problem but I also had mandatory music theory lessons and … concerts.
In my humble opinion, whoever came up with the idea that letting six-year-old children perform difficult and boring classical music in front of bored parents was good for marketing the school, obviously had a few drinks too much.
Of course, I had forgotten everything I hadn't wanted to learn in the first place and the audience tried to be polite, but I felt embarrassed to tears.
And the best was yet to come. Our music school's director thought of himself as a great composer of modern music. Maybe he was, I have no idea.

By modern, I don't mean Rock or Pop or something like that.

I mean modern classical orchestra music with singing that felt like going over five octaves and texts like: winter, wiiiiinter, cold, coming, oh cooooming, wind, ice, dancing, daaancing, ... you get the drift. A Japanese Haiku has more syllables and a better story than the eight pages of lyrics together. And of course, I had to sing it. It didn't matter that they told me left and right that I couldn't sing. Great pedagogical teaching by the way, not.

After the first one or two concerts, I did everything to not have to sing there ever again. I begged my mother to write me an excuse note. For the next seven years, my great-uncles or one of my grandfathers had their 70s or 80s birthday every year. There were more birthdays than I had relatives.

Despite all this, I joined a church band. Our priest tried to modernize our church and a young man, doing community service there and being a drummer in a band, established a church band with children and teenagers from around.

I played flute and it was fun, the young man stayed on as our teacher and leader even after his service and the band grew with some really good musicians.

We even earned some pocket money playing at christenings. The church community wasn't so into us as we played more modern church songs, but they got used to us, mostly. Critics are everywhere.

But life is life and our band leader married and moved away. Our new leader had a different view on this project and a flute wasn't what he wanted. A flute seems not to be a serious instrument for humans over the age of ten. Why did no one ever tell this Ian Anderson from Jethro Tull or bands like Schandmaul and the thousands of paying people in the audience?

As we didn't have enough singers at that time, our new leader put who he could spare in the position behind the microphone.
Take a good guess.
Yes, that meant me. Me with a microphone didn't work out so well, which I could have told him before. I left the band a little later as I didn't feel welcome anymore.

And then I got a new hobby. Martial Arts, especially sword-fighting.
I love swords, still do.
With time I changed from Japanese and Chinese swords to European medieval swords and with a partner and our group we participated at medieval markets all over Germany, which was still a new thing at the time. As we wanted to get better, my partner and I started learning stage combat from different stage combat directors. Two from the Shakespearean Theater in London, who later offered to train us to become stage combat directors ourselves, two from the movie Troy with Brad Pitt, and one from the Lord of the Rings.

Life was great.
I loved being on stage, as one of maybe ten semi-professional sword-fighting women in Germany at that time.
I loved the audience and the applause. It didn't matter that it rained half the time, and we froze our behinds off, we always had a good time on stage. ... And I had a few drunk male fans off stage who could have been my grandfathers at that time. All part of fame, I guess.
I had a few really great years. And I still miss them. They didn't last. I had to find a paying job and my partner got transferred to another country. Also, sadly with no training partner and no money I couldn't finish my training to become a stage combat director.

I do know both sides of the story and I got lucky, my early experiences didn't rob me of all the fun that I had later.
So, for me, I want you to be able to feel all the fun, the lights, the applause that is currently denied to you. And I want you to succeed in whatever you do and maybe live the life that I never had by earning enough money by being on stage. So that you can live your dreams by being a great performer. And maybe I'll be in the audience one day cheering.

And if you are not there yet, maybe you are still too young or still struggling with finding something that works for you, I want you to just have fun and feel the freedom that I felt whenever I changed into my costume. The stage is a different world, and you are a magician who changes everyone's feelings for the better. You are the one who makes people laugh or cry. I want you to feel this magic and soar. It is one of the best feelings that you can ever have.

"If it's a monster, we made it that
way."
— Shane Arbuthnott, Dominion

Chapter 3
About this book

How this book is built.

Here you will find a short explanation of the topics I will talk about in this book.
I would prefer for you to read this book from the beginning to the end at least once, just to have all the necessary background information, that makes this easier and more logical for you. For many people logic is important and everything in your head is not really something I would call logical. Well, it is, but not if you haven't studied it for a while.
If you are going through this book a second or third time, feel free to go to the chapters you need.

So, after this explanation, you will get my side on why I chose this title, what it stands for, and what I want to achieve with this.

Then in Part I, we start with all the logical stuff. First off with how your mind works and then we have a better look at what stage fright is.
Therefore, we need a short excursion in the field of fears, what different kinds of fears there are, and why you suffer from stage fright.

In Part II, I give you the help you were looking for.
As everyone is a little different and everyone has different preferences, I'll give you three methods you can try and see how you like them. Two should show immediate results and the third is to build on top of the other ones.
Later on, I will hand you some other help which I split into common advice for stage fright that you can find everywhere and then some not-so-common advice from my deep hypnotherapy tool bag. All of these small things you can do in between.

One of the things I will also explain to you is hypnotherapy, which is my profession, and it is a really interesting subject that can help you in the area of your stage life but also in many other areas of your life.

It is a great thing to have in your life's toolbox and makes life immensely easier. Many very famous artists use hypnotherapy not because they have problems but because they want to give peak performances again and again.
So, in this chapter, I try to answer all the questions you have about that and maybe tell you a story about a famous person or two who went to one of my teachers for help.
And you will get a little bonus from me if you make it this far in the book. I hope it will floor you.

Last but not least, some ideas on how to go on from here, what you can do, where you can get more information and materials, and how you can reach me if you want to learn more about me, my books, and hypnotherapy.

And then of course some Thank Yous and a little request for you from me.

So, let's start your journey into a better and more fun life by turning this page or sweeping from right to left, whatever the case may be for you.

Why this title

A Little Book of Horrors and How to Deal with Them. What's it with the title of this series?
If it sounds familiar to you, you were either around in the 80s or you like old cheesy horror movies, or both. And yes, we are getting older but the 1980s were hands down the best time ever. If you weren't around, you missed out on something.
Remember the movies Gremlin 1 + 2 and The Little Shop of Horrors? There was also a beautifully drawn Japanese Manga called Pet Shop of Horrors by Matsuri Akino. They were in a way my inspiration for this series.
They all match in one thing.
Someone got something they wanted or desired because it is cute, costly, useful, something everyone who wants to be someone needs, etc. but they didn't read the fine print on their contract or the manual that came with it (who does?) and then did something stupid like feeding the thing after midnight or getting it in contact with water. And boom, they had created a really horrible thing that destroyed their lives, and they didn't know how to get rid of it until in the end the wise shop owner showed up and helped them out.

What has this to do with your stage fright?
You wanted fun and admiration, right?
Maybe success.
Because they are one of the best things ever. Being on stage, being famous. Playing music in front of thousands of people or having a starring role in a movie that could be your door to fame.
And you nearly got it because you have it all, talent, grit, motivation. However, somewhere along the rainbow, something got wrong. And now you are sitting here with that horror of stage fright, and you just want to get rid of it. But you don't know how.
Let me stand in place of the shop owner. Let me help you and even show you how to recycle that awful thing so that it can become something new and beautiful again (The last one is a little bonus that you only get when you read through until the end. And it is for men only, sorry ladies. However, if you are a woman and you have any ideas about what I could give you instead, please contact me).

You are feeling awful right now because you haven't read the manual. Maybe you never got it. And no one ever told you what to effectively do, when you have to go out there and bring it. Not your parents and none of your teachers. I don't think they didn't tell you on purpose. They just never were in the same situation or don't know it themselves.

What I want to achieve with this book

What I really, really want is to give you this manual that you never received, which should have been your birthright.
No one should suffer from stage fright. It is totally unnecessary.

As one cool guy with pointed ears once said: Live long and prosper. That is what I want for you, and I will add my own line. I want you to rock your own world.

Part I

Every time your mind shifts, your
world shifts. - Byron Katie

Chapter 4

About your mind

Before we get into your problem, you need a little knowledge about how your brain works.

You have probably heard the names of some famous psychologists like Sigmund Freud or Carl Jung. There were others and every one of them had a slightly different theory about what goes on in your brain. If you open up your head, you will find a strange gray squishy matter. But you couldn't figure out how it works. Here, I want to introduce you to a theory that works really well, and most psychologists can agree with it, even when they use different terms. We hypnotherapists use this theory as well.
Your brain is divided into two parts. One, we call your conscious mind, the other unconscious mind.

The conscious mind is your actual awareness, the things you consciously see, hear, taste, etc. The things you think when you are concentrating on something. Your conscious decisions like do I go out for lunch or not.
If I go out, I have to pay XX, as I am a little low on money, cooking something for myself would be cheaper, so I stay at home. I could microwave a pizza and watch TV, there is this new series on TV with this great looking actor, what was his name, and haven't I read somewhere that... These things.
Some would say the conscious mind is "me". The music I like, the food I like to eat or not to eat, the clothes I wear, the dreams I have, …

Now, this should be a big part of yourself, right? Nope, wrong. It is really small.
It is actually the unconscious mind that makes up 95% of your brain.
It is running "you". It makes sure you breathe and your heart beats. It tells your body to fight illness, to move your fingers, to blink your eyelashes. It makes your blood flow or clump together, but it also makes decisions in such a short amount of time, you can hardly measure it.
Your brain gets around 11 million bits of information every second through your eyes, ears, nose, mouth and your largest organ, your skin. And it processes and shuffles through it within nanoseconds, deciding what is important and what is not.

And the information that is not needed at this moment is stored somewhere in your brain and forgotten until it is needed again.
Your conscious mind by comparison can only hold and process 40 to 50 bits of information per second.
So, before you even make a conscious decision your background computer races through its data storage looking at your bank account statement the last time you saw it calculating what it could be now. It is looking at your cash in your wallet, the weather, the time you have to be back, the amount of gasoline that should be in your car, what's in the freezer and a hundred more things before you say I'll stay at home. It is kind of handy to have around. Most of the time anyway but not always.

See, the problem with your unconscious mind is, that it is old, doesn't like change, is living it safe and it hasn't gotten the memo yet that we are now living in the 21st century and you are an adult.
And as speech is a thing that constantly changes and is influenced by culture and many other things, your unconscious mind communicates through feelings.

And herein lies the trouble. We never got the manual for our unconscious mind and the dictionary for our feelings. We and our unconscious mind are trying to communicate with each other for thousands of years and still haven't gotten the hang of it. Our unconscious mind is sometimes screaming at us to do or not do something, mostly the latter. But we don't listen and then later we say, oh, I've had this feeling in my stomach, but I did this and that anyway. In hindsight, that was really stupid.
Do you know what that was? That was what we call intuition. It is actually so much more than that. It was your unconscious mind going through mountains of information, checking everything it had twice and telling you that this decision is to 99.9% dangerous. Stay away! YOU HEAR ME?
Of course, you didn't. Up until a few minutes ago you probably didn't even know that you had some part in you that was doing that.

Now that you do have some basic knowledge of what is really going on in your head, let's go back to square one and what your unconscious mind has to do with stage fright. A little hint, it has something to do with communication, feelings and not listening.
And when I talk about the mind, I mean your unconscious mind.

"You are not being judged,

the value of what you are bringing

to the audience is being judged."

- Seth Godin

Chapter 5
About Stage Fright

Stage fright belongs as the name already tells us, to fears, phobias, and anxiety. It is often covered by one of the most common fears which is the fear of public speaking.
The good thing about that is, that fears, phobias, and anxiety are actually really easy and fast to get rid of.
In a while, I will tell you, what helps to reduce them significantly, so that you can function, and if you still want to work on getting rid of them, then I give you another option.

Fear of public speaking or glossophobia affects nearly 75% of adults and is one of the most common treatable fears. It is said that even Cicero, the famous Roman orator suffered from it.

Stage fright is a little bit more specific.

To quote from Wikipedia:
"Stage fright or performance anxiety is the anxiety, fear, or persistent phobia that may be aroused in an individual by the requirement to perform in front of an audience, real or imagined, whether actually or potentially (for example, when performing before a camera). Performing in front of an unknown audience can cause significantly more anxiety than performing in front of familiar faces. [...] Quite often, stage fright arises in a mere anticipation of a performance, often a long time ahead. It has numerous manifestations: stuttering, tachycardia [meaning a racing heart], tremor in the hands and legs, sweaty hands, facial nerve tics, dry mouth, and dizziness."
Later, other symptoms are mentioned like blushing, nausea, and stomach pains. It also affects your digestive system, meaning, you need a bathroom really fast, and your sexual organs, mostly in erectile dysfunction in men, tunnel vision, or a temporary loss of hearing. Many people desire to escape or leave the scene. They are afraid of being rejected or judged.

Whenever you fear something, it doesn't matter what it is, your brain automatically goes into the so-called fight and flight mode. This term is not exactly correct as it doesn't include all possibilities, so it got extended to include the freeze and the faint respectively fawn response.

Fear gets triggered in the oldest parts of your brain, stemming back from the beginning of humanity and even further as animals show the same responses.

Why is fear helpful

We could argue that fear is not a helpful thing, especially when freezing before a performance or in other circumstances before a job interview or talking to someone you fancy, when you make a fool out of yourself by looking like a tomato, stuttering and your stomach dropping down two floors.
However, fear is a bit more primitive than that.
Imagine being back in hunter-gatherer times, when sable-tooth tigers roamed, and mammoths stomped the earth.

Imagine you and your tribe were sitting around a fire in your camp and suddenly a huge tiger steps out of the dark and into your fire's light. What would you do?

Have you ever been in a circus where they had tigers and lions? Even before they come into the arena you can smell them.
They have a distinct big cat smell. A predator's smell. In this second your brain goes into overdrive. Your freeze.
The audience, even the children who were hyperactive a minute before, are completely still. You can hear a pin drop.

Everybody hunkers down, making themselves as small as possible and you can smell the acid fear.

Back to you and your tribe sitting around a fire. The tiger steps up and your brain is calculating your odds of survival in record time. You have only a few options.

Option one is to fight. Not a good idea when a tiger is breathing in your face right now. Its teeth are probably sharper and longer than any weapon you have on you, and even bullets which weren't around yet of course, wouldn't have done much good, more the opposite as in angering it. So, to fight is out.

The next option is flight. Do you know the bad joke about what to do when a bear attacks you? Answer: Running faster than the other person you are with.
Outrunning a tiger is stupid. You can't. And as a tiger is a cat with a strong hunting urge, the first who twitches is dead.

That leaves only fawn or freeze.
Fawning can be an option if the tiger is not exactly in front of you because of the twitching, pouncing, and dead thing. But fainting a little further away could work as it makes you seem unhealthy. Tigers don't eat meat that seems spoiled and could be poisonous or carry illness. At least not when they have other options.

Only one thing left. Freezing. Be as still as possible and hope that the tiger is not too hungry, only curious.

Have you ever watched an animal documentary, where a lion or a cheetah hunted down a gazelle? You know the one that I mean. While the cat has the gazelle's neck in its mouth, some hyenas annoy the cat in hopes of getting the kill without having to hunt for it. They are getting more courageous every time until the cat gets so irritated that it opens its muzzle to click its teeth at the annoying pack. Within a nanosecond, the not-so-dead gazelle springs up on its feet and runs as fast as it can until it is out of reach of both the cat and the hyenas. Then it shakes itself and starts grassing while the cat and the hyenas are trying to make sense of what just happened.

That is a perfectly executed freeze mode. Play dead until you see a chance, get into flight mode by using all the adrenaline the body produced in the meantime, and when you are not in danger anymore, get rid of the remaining adrenaline by shaking, so it won't cause any harm in the body and go on with your life as nothing had ever happened. But hopefully, you have learned a lesson so that this won't happen a second time when no hyenas are around.

Sadly, humans are not as resilient as gazelles.

From a logical point of view, there is nothing to fear by going on a stage and performing in front of an audience. If the audience is your family, they should be nice to you regardless of your performance outcome. If your audience is strangers, they probably already paid to see you. And why do you care what other people think about you anyway?
Unfortunately, reality is different, and fear is not logical, let's not even start with logic and your unconscious mind.

About learned fear

Something to give you hope.
Stage fright is a learned fear like most fears. And everything that is learned, can be unlearned.

Only a very few fears, depending on whom you talk to, are inborn fears. They are natural and everyone has them to a degree. They will not go away but you can build coping mechanisms against them if you need them.
Those fears are the fear of falling (not to be confused with the fear of heights which is learned) and the fear of loud noises. I also heard about the fear of getting something in your eyes as being inborn, which makes sense.
Those fears are there to protect you, even when you are only a small toddler. First, they scream at you to be careful and not do that. If you don't listen, your mind takes over and reacts automatically.

If you were stupid enough to go near something you can fall down from and are not listening to your fear and you fall, to not die your body rolls itself into a ball to increase your chances of survival. Babies and drunks often get fewer injuries than other people would in the same situation. With drunks, the alcohol stops logical thinking, and your unconscious mind reacts automatically. The second you start thinking however, you are a goner.

Fear of loud noises makes someone either keep still and alert or reacting appropriately as fast as they can, depending on the situation. Hearing a tiger roar nearby makes you either freeze or run and hearing a gun shot, you hopefully drop to the ground or search for cover.

As to the third fear, which could be inborn, whenever something comes near your eye, you blink to protect it. You wouldn't want a bee flying into your eye or sand scratching your cornea. Your sight is too precious for that.

All fears have a reason as to why they exist. Some come built in when you were born, and some your mind creates because you seem to be too stupid to act reasonably. At least that is what your mind thinks. Let's find out what stage fright does for you.

What does stage fright do for you

Stage fright is a learned fear, meaning that in your past something happened once or more times to make you wary of performing and having an audience. One can be enough, like it often happens with fear of dogs. One bite is enough to learn to stay away from them forever.
You don't have to remember the situation that caused this, sometimes it is so embarrassing that your mind protects you by forgetting about it. Forgetting doesn't mean it never happened. It is just buried deep inside your mind.
And as your mind likes you, it swore to protect you from any similar situation. Kind of cute, isn't it? Sadly, your mind's options are a little limited.

Your unconscious mind responds as it wants to help protect you, making you fear a certain situation. Its job is to protect you from failure and embarrassment.
It hints to you days in advance that going on stage maybe, perhaps, possibly could be disastrous. You are starting to worry; the pictures are getting more and more detailed, bigger and negative as time goes by and you still haven't decided to cancel that damn concert.

So, your mind ranks up the fear; but you don't listen and are still going near the stage where failure could happen.
So, your mind throws everything it has at you.
You are getting nauseous, can't see and hear well anymore, you shake, and your feet are glued to the floor. You-will-not-go-there!! You shall not pass!!

In your mind's mind, it is your only friend, and it helps you. It doesn't care that it is overreacting. Or that you need the money that comes from performing. Or that you actually like performing.
Your problem now is that the fear and anxiety you feel at this moment will embarrass you even more than the original problem ever had. You are not seven years old anymore and the school bully is now either your best drinking buddy or in jail or in a hospital because he bullied the wrong person.

So, what to do?
Before I give you some exercises to do, a little fact that you should think about.

About roller coasters

From a biological point of view, your body's reaction to fear and excitement is the same.
Your body creates the same chemical reactions when you are afraid and when you are excited.
Take a roller coaster for example.
Some people love it and some hate it.
When you are driving up the incline, your body creates adrenaline and other stuff in your body that helps you deal with whatever comes.
On top of the incline, there is a very short amount of time, when you decide to either look forward and like it or to worry and hate it. This is where you decide.
No one and nothing, not even your own mind can really make you interpret your own feelings. Only when you don't do it yourself, your mind will take over and decide for you. And because it is an overreacting, clucking old mother hen, it decides that fear is always appropriate.
Now you hate roller coasters. You are not going near them, and your mind is padding itself on its imaginary shoulder telling itself good job, possible disaster avoided.

Take Bruce Springsteen and Carly Simon for example. They both suffered from stage fright.

The only difference is that Bruce Springsteen told himself that he wanted to go out there.
He overcame his fear of performing in front of an audience.
Sadly, Carly Simon never did.
She reduced her public performances to a bare minimum.

There are lots of stars, musicians, actors, and other entertainers alike, who suffered or are still suffering from stage fright.
With musicians, it is a bit more obvious. Let's see who you would have never thought to have that issue.
Someone I would have never guessed to have a problem on stage is Rod Steward. Not him. He's been on stage for ages. But yes, he suffers from stage fright.
At the beginning of her career, Cher always wanted a partner on stage, so that she could look at them and not at the audience. With time it seemed to have become better and now she even enjoys doing Broadway shows.
Ozzy Ozbourne wrote about his stage fright in his autobiography and Eddy Van Halen never got over it and tried to fight it by drinking alcohol before a show. By the way, alcohol never works in the long run.
Going to more current musicians like Adele, Rhianna, and Kate Perry are not only on top of the charts but also on top of the list of having issues with stage fright.

Of course, people outside the Rock and Pop scene also suffer from this fear.
Take the Opera stage for example.
Luciano Pavarotti, called one of the best tenors of all time, always muttered that he was going to his death before he stepped on stage.
Andrea Bocelli, the blind opera singer, who is adored all over the world, thinks he can never fulfill the audience's expectations.
And pianist Vladimir Horowitz' perfectionism drove him into an excruciating stage fright and in the end into retirement from the stage because he felt always under stress.

So, you are in good company. Can you be a great entertainer and get famous even while suffering from stage fright?
As you can see above, you can. But why should you? It is much more fun and better for your health to just get rid of it. Start by deciding that what you are feeling is excitement. It probably won't be the first time or the second but keep on doing it. Fake it till you make it or better until you have convinced your mind that you really want this. That you choose to do this.

If you need more convincing yourself, see it from your audience's perspective.
There are some people who hold on to their opinion that entertainers are a sign of a decadent society. They are not needed and only a disturbance to good working citizens.

Sadly, they can't see behind their own thoughts.
Entertainers of all kinds are needed.
We can discuss the topics they are transferring or the way they behave but if they sell their goods, there are customers who want or need them, even when other people don't agree. So, you are actually giving something to society and it is all right to get paid for your service.
What do I mean by that?

What entertainers do for society

Let's start again with musicians. It is widely recognized that music can heal your soul. As a fun fact depending on the music, it makes cows produce more milk.
Anyway, musicians and especially singers give people their voice. Not everyone can sing or is allowed to sing. But listening to someone sing, you can sing with them in your head. Music makes people live out their feelings. In a concert, they can cry, shout and scream. Something that is not acceptable in public. But feelings need to be felt, otherwise, you end up getting sick, either physically or mentally. They need to get out.
Death Metal may not be your favorite music to listen to, but they have a huge following, especially in countries where there isn't so much sun and the government is putting Omega-3-Oil into everything to fight against depression.
If music helps keep people mentally stable by allowing them to live their feelings in an acceptable way and they choose themselves, I will say all power to music.

Similar to actors. Actors are telling a story. They act out different roles one can either identify with or hate.

They bring us into another world. One where all our problems are forgotten for a while.
Where there is someone who has even worse difficulties in life than you and overcomes them. You can learn from that.

Stories are important on stage and in books.
Once when I was living in a shared flat, my flatmate only read books where at the end tragedy strikes and everyone dies. She told me, for her, that is what reality is and so she only reads this. She identified with those characters and learned from them for occasions in her own life. Which I hope will never come for her. No one needs tragedy.
Me, I only read books with a happy ending because that is what I want out of life. And when life won't give me that, at least I had them in my books.
It shouldn't come as a surprise that we never shared books.

Other than that, comedians make you laugh, dancers make you dance and fly. Even satirists have their worth.
The jury is still out of the necessity of critics but then they are not entertainers, aren't they?

As you now know why you should be going on stage for yourself and for others and have fun with it, I will show you what you can do to accomplish exactly that.

Part II

"The best advice I can give to anyone going through a rough patch is to never be afraid to ask for help."
— Demi Lovato, Stay Strong

Chapter 6

About Immediate Help

In this chapter, I will show you three techniques, one old, but you probably haven't heard of it before, one brand new, and one you can use to build up onto the other two.
All can help you in the moment you are afraid. And I am not only speaking about stage fright. They work with all fears, whenever you are afraid of something.
But they need some preparation, so you should have done them a time or two before you go on stage.

About One-Point

The first technique comes originally from Martial Arts. I knew it before my hypnotherapist trainer taught it to us, I just never thought about this technique as being helpful outside of Martial Arts. Of course, I forgot that the old masters knew more about the body and psyche than what is taught in many dojos nowadays. Chinese medicine was big in old times.
If you have ever watched something along the lines of Karate Kid, you have seen this technique in action.
We call it One Point.

First, I will tell you how to do One-Point, and later, I will explain to you what it does in your body and mind.

Read through the exercise. You can either read through it from beginning to end and then practice or read it step by step adjusting on the go. For your first try, it doesn't matter.
It would be helpful to have someone assist you in the beginning, but you can do it without help.

Exercise:

1) Stand in a place, where you have a little room around you and are not feeling pressed by clutter.
Now, conjure up the feeling of stage fright you have. On a scale from 1-10, with 1 being nothing and 10 having a full-blown panic attack, where you are right now?
Let go of the fear and clear your mind.

2) Now either close your eyes or stare into the distance, stand strong on your feet, your feet hip distance apart, you don't need to go into a deep fighting stance, but go a little into your knees and concentrate on the middle of your body, around your navel. If you have someone to help you, let them click their fingers a little in front of your navel. That makes it easier for you to find the spot. You can lay your hand on your stomach if this helps you concentrating.

3) If you are alone, just concentrate on your breathing and on the area around your navel. Maybe get a little more into a kind of riding seat stance at least in your mind, you don't have to do that in reality. Check in your number from time to time to see if it has dropped down a number already. If not, continue concentrating on your stance and on your breathing until it does.

If you have help, let them push a little from the side (A little!!) against one of your shoulders, while you are holding against it, concentrating on you navel and breathing. If you wobble, let them click their fingers in front of your navel and then push again, until you got it and can stay strong. Then they can push more.
Let your help ask if your feeling has dropped down a number. Concentrate on you middle part of your body until the number drops.
If you are alone, you can imagine someone pushing you from the side of your shoulder.

4) Repeat until the number drops to a tolerable level.

5) When you feel strong and calm, open your eyes or focus them again and come back into your reality.
Now, on a scale from 1-10, where is your feeling now? Try to conjure it up again.

6) If your feeling is still around five, do it again until it drops to 2-3. This should be tolerable.

7) Thank your help if you had one. Then thank yourself for doing something for you.

Now I will do something, that Martial Arts trainers normally don't do. I will explain to you, what you are doing as I know, this exercise looks a little stupid and how on earth does this help?

I will borrow from different systems, to make it easier for you to follow.

If you are familiar with Yoga, you may have heard about chakras. There are seven main chakras, one of them is called manipura chakra, the navel chakra. This is the one we are working with. It's element is fire and it is seen as the seat of our personality. Here you can achieve changes in your goals and feelings. By activating it as we do through breathing into it and concentrating on it, we also activate our confidence and self esteem, increase our willpower and it gives us a little feeling of happiness.

The clicking in front of your stomach is done to get you out of your head. When you are afraid, you are only in your head and not grounded anymore. Your fight and flight takes over and you are getting unstable in your stance so you can bolt anytime. In this moment even very little outside pressure can shove you over.

So to get you back in harmony and balance with your body, you need to concentrate on your navel area, which is also the center point of your body. When your body is in harmony, your mind is, too. They influence each other.
Something you can make use of when you are afraid. I will tell you more about that in a later chapter.

The feet hip distance apart and sitting a little lower in your hips is a grounding method from Martial Arts. Tai Chi for example uses it a lot. Staying strong in this pose makes it very difficult for someone else to push you over, even when the other person is taller, heavier and stronger than you. Again, it sends a message to your brain that you are strong and not afraid.

The pressure from outside, when someone pushes you a little on your shoulder, keeps you focused on staying on balance and out of your head.

With all these body signs of balance and strength, your mind follows suit and your fear drops. And the best part your mind remembers that you reacted to fear with being calm and centered and changes it's opinion to it. You don't seem to mind, so the mind won't mind either.

Repeat this a few times at home and do it before you go on stage and it will go easier and faster every time. After a few times you only need to take a deep breath and focus on your stomach and you will feel calm or depending on your preparation and the level of stage fright, at least calmer. And when you feel calm, you can decide to feel exited. And when you feel exited, you can have fun.
Let's move on to an even more powerful technique, that is easy to do and can help you within minutes.

About Havening®

Havening® is a psychosensory technique, meaning it uses sensory input like touch, sound, and sight to change your thoughts, moods and behaviors. So far it helped with a huge range of problems from fears and phobias, chronic pain, anger, panic attacks, PTSD, victims of natural disasters or man-made events like war, gravings, emotional eating. Therefor stage fright is not a big deal for it.
The word Havening® stems from the phrase "a safe haven".
If you want to read more on Havening®, the studies about it or testimonials go to havening.org. I've put the link in the Resources Section of this book.

In this book we will use one form of Havening® called Event Havening®. It was made public and free of charge during the Covid pandemic as a way of helping medical and care personnel to get through this stressful time. It is also easy to use on yourself without the help of a professional.

Event Havening® here entails that the stressor that triggered your problem is a one-time event in your past. So for us that means you are concentration on one stage fright episode at a time. One should be enough but later on you can also work on different episodes if you want to.
For ongoing events like for example everyday bullying another technique would be used. But if you are in such a situation and don't have anything else at hand, you could at least haven on particular bullying situations in the past. That could also help and change your emotional state reflecting it on the outside. Just try it, it can't hurt.

I used Event Havening® on myself on multiple occasions and it always worked like a charm and very fast.

What does Havening® do

I wouldn't want you to use something as profound as this without explaining to you what it does in your mind. It is not magic and no Voodoo. It is pure science.

Normally, when you have an event A, your mind answers with reaction B. If it works, meaning you survived or even got something else out of it, your brain memorizes this way of reaction. If something similar as A occurs, your brain goes straight to reaction B. You may have heard the German term "never change a running system" before. In English, it would translate into "if it ain't broke, don't fix it".

This could look like this. A small child is in a supermarket and wants some ice cream. The parent says no. What does the child do? It throws itself on the floor and starts a temper tantrum in a sound volume that would make the bands Kiss and Manowar, the loudest bands on earth, green with envy.
What does the parent do? It gives the child it's ice cream to make it stop.
Event A: I want something and don't get it.
Reaction B: I throw a temper tantrum and get it.
Great. Works. Lesson learned.

Fast forward 20 to 40 years.

You want to go on your dream holiday but your partner says no because it is too expensive and would put you in debt for a long time.

Your brain trained to react within a nanosecond does what? Yes, it throws a temper tantrum and for good measure throws some dishes at your partner, too.

Does it work? Maybe, that depends on your partner. If it does, then only with great disgust on your partner's side and probably not a second time. If your partner has any backbone, you just took a big step toward a breakup.

And … it was childish and immature as hell. You are not a 3-year-old in a supermarket anymore.

In your brain, it looks like this.

Think about A and B as destinations or places in your brain. To go from A to B the electrical impulses in your brain, see them as small messengers on horses, travel a road. If you use B often, then the road is well traveled and gets broader and clearer, and you can find this road on any map in your brain.

But if you don't want reaction B anymore, maybe C sounds better, then what to do? Use Havening®.

What Havening® does is to confuse or even totally erase the road. Depending on the size of the road one Havening® session may be enough to totally erase it, sometimes you need more, so your messengers can't find their way to B anymore and go back to A, asking where to bring their message.

Now that gives you a second to breathe and think of another reaction that would be more appropriate.

When you have decided, your little messengers go happily on their way to this new destination because they don't care where they go, they just do their job. It may take a while because your maps aren't up to date and the roads aren't clear yet, you wouldn't want the horse to stumble and break a leg, would you? But eventually, they find their way faster and faster. And your reaction becomes ingrained.

This not only works with reactions but also with feelings, which are a kind of reaction on their own.

Let's imagine you just got a letter saying your contract got canceled or you didn't get the role you were hoping for. This would be event A. Now you normally react with B, falling to your knees, dissolving into a puddle of tears, and seeing your world end.

Wouldn't it be a better reaction to take a deep breath, curse a bit, accept it and then move on? Other possibilities may open and who knows, the production of this movie could crash, or the media could tear apart the role you wanted and it would have been the end of your career before it actually started.

So, whenever you feel overwhelmed by a feeling you don't want to feel, start havening. It levels out your emotion.
It won't make you happy. I am honest with you here. It only makes your devastating feelings go in the direction of Zero. You are calm. From there you can choose something different but for me being calm and kind of content is actually a good thing. And it is just a small step from there to feeling happiness again, if you choose so. But it is your choice now.

A little caution here. It doesn't only erase bad feelings. It also erases or levels out good ones. I once used it on my feelings for a guy who broke up with me and after using the havening technique for a while, I couldn't remember some things about him anymore. That is what I mean by that. I still know that I loved him and that we had good times, but they became a little blurry. It is, what normally happens with time. You forget. The saying "Time is a great healer" is accurate. Havening® just does it faster for you.

But now I don't want to stop you anymore from getting well again. Here we go (not "again on my own" but this time with help. If you don't understand my little joke, it was a bad one, sorry. And listen to Whitesnake.).

How to haven

I want you to read the following exercise from the beginning to the end. And only when you have understood and memorized the sequence of the eight steps, actually do it. You need to concentrate on yourself and not squint at the text. Ready?

1) Call up the event or feeling you want to change. Go into it and feel it again. On a scale from 1 to 10 with one being no problem to ten devastating, where is your feeling now?

2) Clear your mind and lay your right hand on your left shoulder and your left hand on your right shoulder. Then stroke your hands down your arms to your palms. Do that again and again. Don't stop.

3) Now whilst still stroking down your arms close your eyes and imagine you are on a beach. You can feel the sand under your feet, feel the warmth of the sun on your skin, hear the waves coming onto shore and smell the salt in the air.
Start walking down the beach and with each step, count aloud from one to twenty. If you can't talk loudly, do it in your head. When you have counted to twenty…

4) Open your eyes and still stroking your hands down your arms move your eyes from the left to the right and from the right to the left without moving your head. Only move your eyeballs. Do that 4-5 times.

5) Now whilst still stroking down your arms close your eyes and imagine you are in a park. Feeling the grass under your feet, hearing the birds sing, smell the flowers along the way and feeling the gentle warmth of the sun on your face. Start walking in the park and with each step, count aloud from one to twenty. If you can't talk loudly, do it in your head. When you have counted to twenty…

6) Open your eyes and still stroking your hands down your arms move your eyes from the left to the right and from the right to the left without moving your head. Only move your eyeballs. Do that 4-5 times. Then close your eyes again.

7) Still stroking your arms take a deep breath in and let it all go. Open your eyes and stop stroking.

8) Try to get up your feeling again. On a scale from 1 to 10, where is your feeling now?

By now your bad feeling should have been reduced. If you think it is still too high, haven again until it is on a level you are comfortable with.

When it is somewhere under five you can stop for the day if you wish or go on once more.
Do this as often as you need. I havened a lot in the first three days after my breakup, every time my eyes got blurry, I sat down and havened to get all the triggers.

I would recommend to my clients to do this process at least once five days in a row. Then your feeling should be gone or at least down to a comfortable level. Try it, it works differently for everyone depending on the size of your road. There is no right or wrong, only you being content with it.

The version I've written down for you is just one of many as it is evolving and every practitioner tweaks it a little. But I think it is the easiest to remember and works splendidly.

Another option. Most people like the beach and relax thinking about it. The same goes for the image of a park. If you should have trouble with one of them, you can swap it.
I would then use going down a big ballroom staircase feeling my feet on the stairs, the carpet underneath, my hand sliding down the handrail, and the lights overhead.
I would use this image as the second one and something in nature for the first.
So, you can change images if you like. They are not written in stone.

If you have done the technique, you will feel different by now. It works immediately. Havening® is always a good starting point for every fear you have. Now you are good to go on and try some different techniques to overcome your stage fright, if you haven't already.

In the Resources Section I put a link to a video, where Paul McKenna is talking you through the Havening® process, so if you have struggled with your written exercise, watch the video.

About Anchoring

This technique comes from NLP (Neuro-Linguistic Programming). It is easy to do and powerful.
NLP was developed by John Grinder and Richard Bandler in the 70s.
NLP in itself is a very powerful system and tool that can help you immensely with many mental issues. Many professional coaches and hypnotists, including me, use it. It is a tool and as with every tool, the wielder decides if it is good or bad. As this is a self-help book, the wielder is you and you should want only the best for yourself. So, use it.

As the name Anchoring implies, it anchors something. It anchors a feeling. Every time you trigger your anchor, you will feel this feeling. Meaning if you want to be excited, you can anchor the feeling of excitement.
If you want to anchor calmness, you can do that, too.

You can anchor this feeling to a body part, like for example the tip of your right index finger or your left knee. Or you can anchor it to a thing you use, like a special ring. Flowing colorful scarf hanging from a microphone, anyone? It's amaaaaazing. Sorry, bad joke again. The band starts with A by the way.
Or you can anchor to a process like stepping on stage or getting into your stage outfit.
Whatever works best for you.

I wouldn't recommend anchoring it on a musical instrument as you will feel this feeling to a degree every time you touch this thing. It wouldn't be practical to be excited too much while warming up or practicing. The feeling of focusing would work in that case. Think it through before you anchor.

And talking about excitement, you can also anchor a different feeling of excitement (you know what I mean. Wink, wink.), so that you can use it when you are not feeling up to it but don't want to disappoint or are too nervous and are afraid that you won't make a stand otherwise.
Just as a little advice from your friendly hypnotherapist.

A short excursion into the land of acting.
Actors often have to switch emotions fast, from anger to sadness with tears flowing. You can anchor that. Crying on demand works similarly.

You can anchor the feeling on a body part that you can touch without it being seen or you can anchor it to a part of your costume, a wig for example, or a prob if you have access to it in advance.

The method is there. Use it. Other people already do.

How to anchor

Please read through the exercise before you do it, so that you have the process in your head as you probably close your eyes.

1) First, decide what feeling you want to anchor. Anchor only one feeling at a time or it will get muddled and you will lose the anchoring. For this exercise we use excitement.

2) Then decide where you want your anchor. I would recommend using the tip of your index finger by pressing the tip of your thumb to it for your first try. Only anchor one feeling to one body part otherwise the first feeling gets overlapped and canceled out.

3) Conjure up a situation where you felt the feeling you want to feel. Maybe Christmas, being excited and curious about opening your presents.
Make the feeling bigger by giving it a color and brightening it. You can also give it a form, like a ball and make it bigger. And bigger and brighter. And then press your anchoring point. Hold for a few seconds and let go.

4) Conjure up the situation again and make the feeling even stronger. Stronger, you can do it.
And press your thumb to your index finger. Hold a few seconds and let go.

5) Then, come up with a different situation but the same feeling. Maybe you got something you always wanted and are hopping up and down because you are so excited and happy.
Make the feeling bigger, brighter and bolder. You know what to do. Then press your anchor again for a few seconds. Let go.

6) Now you can check if that is enough. This time fire your anchor by pressing onto your fingertip. What do you feel?
If the feeling of excitement comes up strong, you did it. If not, go through the steps again and make sure your good feeling is huge.

Check a few times before you use it in the real situation.
If you need this feeling only for certain times, like on a tour and then you have a break for a few months, check in before the next tour. If it is not used for some time, it can get lost in the everyday use of your anchor. But it should come back fast after you renewed it.

I recommend Anchoring after Havening® or One-Point, so that you are coming from a calmer position. It is more effective that way and easier than working against the fear itself. Whereas your level of fear is higher than your level of excitement, it won't do much help. But if your excitement is higher, your fear could collapse in on itself. The word here is could, as you are probably suffering from a big stage fright. So, level down your feelings first just in case.

If you like this technique, you can also install an internal anchor, so that you don't have to touch anything. But for that, you need a hypnotherapist.
We can anchor your desired feelings to a control panel in your mind, where you only have to switch a lever. If you want to know more, you can contact me at www.andreastrunz.com

"Every day, in every way, I am getting better and better."

–Émile Coué, French psychologist & pharmacist

Chapter 7

About Other Help

There are other small things that can help you with stage fright. They don't stop it, but they help nonetheless. Some of them you might already know, some not.

Common Advice by Stage fright

The most common ones you have probably heard about, are these:

Practice and prepare
Even when your mind gets blank, if you have practiced some movements enough, like playing a song, your mind can do it without you. It becomes automatic. But for you to get to this level you must clock a lot of practice hours.
Speaking or singing is more of a problem as you do it in your mind that just goes blank.

Don't experiment
As long as you tend to be nervous, don't experiment. Stick to what you know.

Train
Go into problematic situation as often as you can.
Start small with entertaining family and friends and then go to street entertainment or small stages. Climb up the ladder bit by bit until you get used to. Depending on your level of fear this can work or not.

Visualize your outcome
What does your ideal outcome look like. How do you move, how do you speak, how does your audience react. Go through this process again and again. Then built in some small problems like technical problems, rain etc. How would you react if this would happen?

You can go through visualization alone or you can ask a hypnotist to guide you through. There are some techniques, mostly NLP, we use for that.
Many sports people, like golf players and many famous musicians use it. It is part of their mental training before a performance.
One musician who uses those and similar visualization techniques is Roger Daltrey from The Who. He already is a great entertainer and has no stage fright, but he uses visualization to up his performance.
He also talks about it and he was a client of my teacher Paul McKenna, so this anecdote is proven. Hypnotherapists do have data protection by the way, so we are not allowed to talk about our clients or their issues. Only when the client goes out there and talks about it publicly, may we use your names.

Visualization is important. Maybe you have heard of the famous basketball study by Dr. Biasiotto at the University of Chicago.
Three groups were training in basketball.

Group 1 trained free throws for one hour every day for one month.
Group 2 trained only in their heads, visualizing. And group 3 didn't train at all.
After one month they compared their progress. Of course, group 3 had none.
Group 1 improved by 24% and the visualization group improved by 23% without ever throwing a ball in reality.
Your mind can't differentiate between reality and imagination. So, make sure your visualization is positive because up to now you only visualized doom, resulting in your stage fright.

Positive Mantras
Use positive affirmation or a mantra like "The audience will love me", "I can do everything I want and I chose this.", "I go out there and have fun". Depending on your level of fear it won't be as effective but after leveling down your stage fright through One-Point or Havening®, use it.

Focus
When you are on stage, focus on one point in the distance or one person in the audience. Depending on the stage lights you won't see much but if you can, choose someone you find attractive or choose some pillar or loudspeaker box and imagine this is your biggest fan. Play only for this person.

At the beginning of her career, Cher only went on stage with her husband Sonny. She got a bad case of stage fright and only looked at him and sang for him. As long as she was in love with him, it worked well.

No coffee and no alcohol
Coffee and alcohol create havoc in your body at the best of times. Both dry out your vocal cords and make it harder to speak or sing. If you still use your voice too much after drinking the stuff, you can seriously damage it.
They also alter your mood by either pushing it (caffeine) or pressing it down (alcohol), which creates another construction side for your body to deal with as if stage fright isn't enough.
Drink water or herb tea a few hours before going on stage. Make sure you are hydrated and eat something healthy and small to have enough energy for performing.

Therapy
Also a point you may have come across. Get yourself a therapist. I would recommend using the immediate help techniques before that, as therapy can be expensive and ongoing for a long time, depending on what kind of therapist you choose. Cognitive-behavioral therapists are often consulted with fear issues. They do show results, but it takes up to at least six months.

Of course, I am a little biased here, but I would recommend hypnotherapy, as the results are coming in much faster. More about that in the chapter about hypnotherapy.

These were the most common things you can do to help you with your issue.
Now let's have another look into my hypnotherapy bag as I do have some other small helpful things for you that are not so common.

Uncommon Advice by Stage fright

In One-Point, we already talked about the collaboration of mind and body. If one does something, it influences the other.

About Body Language

During my time in Japan, I had English cable TV and as I didn't like the Japanese TV program, I was watching the History Channel, Discovery Channel, and Animal Planet up and down.
One program I liked was "The Dog Whisperer" with Cesar Millan. In one episode he explained about fearful dogs.
When a dog is afraid, the dog's body language advertises fear by sticking the tail between the hind legs and pushing down the dog's head.
To get your dog out of it, Cesar Millan advised you to bind a leash around the tail and hold it vertically in the air while walking the dog. After a few steps, the dog's body language changed, and he wasn't so fearful anymore.
Also, you shouldn't pat a dog on the head as it pushes the head down, making the dog uncomfortable. Instead, you should tickle him under his chin, which lifts his head and makes him feel more confident.

Now, of course, we are not dogs and we don't have tails to uplift (and for all my male readers, no, don't go there).
But body language is body language.

What does a person look like when he/she is afraid?
The head is down, and the shoulders are hunched over making the body as small as possible.
We have here a little of a what comes first, the hen or the egg problem. When you hunch over, your body creates body chemistry that activates the fight-flight-freeze mode, and your mind takes over. And the other way, when your mind decides to help you by activating the fight-flight-freeze mode, your body hunches over.

You can try it. Hunch your shoulders forward and tuck your chin under, then wait a moment. How do you feel? At least uncomfortable, right?

Now, every time you feel afraid, or you start to freeze, consciously change your body language. Push your shoulder blades back and your chest out, pull your chin up and stand or sit straight, then monitor your feelings. After a few moments, you will feel better. You just overrode your mind. Use it every time you recognize slipping into fear again.

About opening your wings

Did you ever have charisma lessons? Or maybe some acting lessons?
There is a really nice exercise, that I like a lot. Children especially adore it but most adults, too.
It's called "Open Your Wings". And that's it. Just open your wings.

Now, I know you don't have wings but imagine you do and open them. What happens? You suddenly feel good, and you are standing straight and tall.

I told you before, that your mind can't differentiate between imagination and reality. When you imagine having wings on your back, your back muscles move and as wings are heavy, the muscles pull your spine up and your shoulder blades out, which opens your chest and makes more room to breathe.

If you don't believe me, ask someone else to do it. I bet you can see the exact moment the person does it. The whole atmosphere around that person changes in an instant.

And it doesn't matter what kind of wings you imagine. It can be angel wings, butterfly wings or gargoyle wings.
Use the ones you like the most and which go with the atmosphere you want to create.

Death Metal and pink sparkly butterfly wings don't go together well, I think. But that is just me. By the way, depending on your wingspan and how long you are holding onto your image, it could happen that people are making space for you. Try it, it is fun.

If you are not a wing-type, you can substitute with a golden thread or string that sticks out of the middle of your head. Pull yourself up on it.
It also makes you stand or sit tall, but it won't open your chest so that you can breathe better.
Swallow and short breathing are a symptom of fear. Taking deep and calm breaths is a symptom of confidence.
Personally, I prefer my wings. They are much cooler.

About creating spit

This topic might be a little yuck, but it helps.
When you are afraid, your mouth gets dry as your body redirects every resource it has, blood, water, and so on to a place that helps you escape, like your heart. It also stops processes of things that are not necessary for survival, like your digestion or your sexual drive.
So, to counter your fear, you trick your body into believing that you are not afraid.
You can do this by changing your body language or by creating saliva and swishing it around your mouth.

If your mouth is too dry, use water and swish it around in your mouth. Your mind gets the signal that your mouth is wet and gets confused.
Combine your swishing saliva with changing your body language and your mind gives up. You are not afraid. You know the saying "Fake it till you make it".

"Our client's problem is that they have lost rapport with their unconscious mind. Our job is to help restore that relationship."

–Milton Erickson, American psychiatrist

Chapter 8

About Hypnotherapy

By now you had a first glance into my hypnotherapy bag and maybe you are interested in what more there is. Depending on which country you are from, hypnotherapy is a new concept for you. At least it was for me when I first found out about it on the internet. It is not very well known in Germany but slowly getting there. Also the term may vary depending on the licenses you need in your part of the world. So Hypnotherapist, Hypnotist and Mind Coach could be the same thing. If in doubt, just ask the person.

What is Hypnosis

Many people have a wrong perception of hypnosis. They have mostly seen a TV show from the 80s, heard something about it from friends or know it as a party trick.

There is a difference between Stage Hypnosis and Hypnotherapy. Stage Hypnosis is for show and everything that is done for entertainment is not always what it seems. Believe me, I know, I have been on stage for some time in my life, though not as a hypnotist.
There is certainly some truth in stage hypnosis, but hypnotherapy is not about the laughs, it is about helping people overcome their mental issues.
I already mentioned Paul McKenna, one of my teachers, who was also a stage hypnotist for some time, but now does mostly serious work leading in this field.

So, what is hypnosis? Hypnosis is a natural state of mind. Yes, you have read that correctly. It is natural and you are in a kind of trance a bunch of times each day. Every time you do something automatically, you are in a trance. Can't remember most of your drive? You were in a trance. Looking out of the window daydreaming? A trance.

If you don't like the word trance or hypnosis, use the word deep relaxation, because that's what it is.

The short time between being awake and sleeping is the same state hypnotherapists use. Every night before you fall asleep and every morning before you are awake but not sleeping anymore, you are in a trance.

How Hypnosis works

During this time, when you are not quite awake or asleep yet, your brain waves change and are more receptive. It is now easier to talk to your unconscious mind directly without your conscious mind with its logic standing in between and blocking communication. This is often the only time to "tell" your unconscious mind what you want it to do or the other way round, the only time your unconscious can talk more clearly to you.

For that, it is easiest to go to someone who can hypnotize you. A hypnotist can guide you into deep relaxation and then talk to your unconscious mind or install new beliefs and behaviors while you relax and do nothing.

Hypnosis in itself has been around for a long long time. No one knows how long exactly but there are written records from 4000 years ago, when Sumerian doctors used it. Egyptian and Greek doctors and priests also used something called temple sleep.

If you compare the success rates of hypnotherapy and normal psychotherapy, you will find an enormous difference.

Alfred A. Barrios, Ph.D. conducted a Meta study, meaning he took over 2000 former studies and deduced an overall result from it.

His result was that in 600 hours of normal psychoanalysis, only 38% of clients found a solution to their problem.

In 22 hours of psychotherapy 72% of clients left with a solution, which is way better of course.

But then a whopping 93% of clients left their problem behind after only 6 hours of hypnosis.

I would know where I want to go if I want fast and lasting results.

Is Hypnosis safe

Many clients of hypnotherapy have this concern that they would do something under hypnosis that they wouldn't do when they were awake. That they would embarrass themselves by clucking like a chicken or blurting out secrets.
First of all, don't worry. It is safe. You have a natural built-in firewall in your brain that stops anything that you wouldn't normally do. You do have your values and settings and hypnosis won't go against it.

One of my German hypnotist trainers once told us, that a friend of his, another hypnotist called him, pleading with him to come to Munich ASAP and help him out. He was part of a TV show filming people to do strange things under hypnosis. He was doing stage hypnosis. So, the movie company wanted him to find someone who would go to a cash machine, take out 100€ of their own account, and then burn them in front of the camera after being hypnotized to do that.
Guess what, it didn't work. He couldn't hypnotize anyone to do that. In the end, three hypnotists hypnotized around 600 people to find one guy, who in the end burned his money. And the only reason he did it, was, that 100€ was pocket money for him. He didn't care about it.

So, you can see, if you wouldn't do it awake, you wouldn't do it in a trance.
And please remember, people who are going to a stage hypnosis show want to be hypnotized. They expect to cluck like a chicken. And there is a selection process before the show that you don't see and know about.

Another little story, this time personal. When I was training to become an RTT Therapist, we had a lot of partner training sessions, so I got hypnotized often.
In one of these sessions, my hypnotist tried to help me with a problem but she used some ideas and phrases that were totally against what I was believing. She meant well and spoke from her experience, but I was totally aware of what she was doing, and a feeling of a wall came up, that said no, I don't want that. It blocked everything out.

Another thing, hypnotherapists have a moral code like every doctor or psychologist. Even if we could, we wouldn't do something against your will because we would lose clients and our credibility fast.

There is a slight possibility that after a hypnosis something comes up, that makes a client uncomfortable. That can happen because your brain is still processing and working on the new beliefs and installments, which can take a while.

Let's say you wanted to get rid of stage fright and one of the reasons you are having this is because you were bullied in school when you had to give a talk.
After your hypnosis session, your brain is still searching and throwing out random other events that had something to do with your problem.
Like your yearly family event where they make the children sing something and then laugh and make fun of it, which can be really cruel for the child.

Your mind is in a way like a dog that proudly brings you something it has found. Sometimes those memories are not good. If you experience something like this, it will either go away by itself in a day or two, just be patient and tell your mind thank you, but I don't need this anymore – it does work, and your brain has no trouble doing what it is told – or speak to your hypnotherapist again.

I think I can't be hypnotized

This is mostly a wrong belief in what hypnosis looks like. You have seen people on TV, that were lolling around in their chairs, oblivious to anything that was going on around them.

Contrary to popular belief, being in a trance doesn't mean you are in a coma and helpless. Many clients are even disappointed after a session because they think they haven't been hypnotized. Their expectation differed from reality.

Back to one of my former explanations. Hypnosis is a natural state of mind, you are in a trance many times each day whether you want it or not. You can't survive for long without falling asleep.
And what most hypnotists use is only a light or a middle trance. You are not going deep. You can still hear everything around you and you can wake up any minute if you wanted to or had to because of an emergency.
That's why we ask you to turn off your mobile phone and make sure no one else is around, so you can concentrate on yourself. Light trances are enough, and we use body indicators to make sure that you are in a trance.

Letting go of logic and trusting your hypnotherapist has a lot to do with your motivation to get rid of your problem. If you don't really want to or when someone else makes you go to a session, your results will be pretty low. Again, we can't and we won't manipulate you. Why would we? It is your life and your decision. There are enough people that want our help.

There are indeed some people that are harder to hypnotize. They still can be hypnotized but your hypnotist needs a lot of patience and experience and probably a few more sessions than normal to gain enough trust. You will find those harder to hypnotize people often in professional soldiers or policemen, who were trained to withstand torture and brainwashing, so they have in a way some trust issues.
Some other people are naturally harder to hypnotize but they are very rare. The possibility of winning a 10-million-dollar jackpot is much higher than not being able to be hypnotized.

Richard Bandler always says something like this: "I don't give up. We stay here and try until one of us is dead and it won't be me." So, if you are one of these rare people, find a hypnotherapist with a lot of patience but remember, you have to pay for the sessions. It will be cheaper for you to give up resisting. Do you want to be right, or do you want to stop suffering? Whatever you want will happen. You decide.

What Hypnosis can do for you

Hypnosis is a tool to help people overcome their mental problems.

It works great with fears and phobias of all kinds, anxiety, and worries, getting more confident, becoming more positive, getting more motivation, overcoming procrastination, helping with creativity, sleep problems, getting pregnant, having an easier birth, helping with your weight, getting rid of addictions like smoking, sexual problems and many more.

Some of these issues are covered by most hypnotherapists, just ask them if they do that.

For others a specialist is preferable.

There are also some issues, like treatment for children, eating disorders or depression, where you absolutely want to go to a specialist.

Also in some countries, like Germany, or states, like in America, special licenses are necessary to help with some things.

Even fear is something not everyone is allowed to work with without a special license. So, when you are diagnosed with fear, ask your hypnotherapist beforehand if he is allowed to handle that.

If you are not diagnosed by a doctor or psychologist, just knowing that you are afraid of something, playing it safe by using the word panic or fright is advisable. It has nothing to do with the competence of your hypnotist but with law and lobby work.

What hypnosis doesn't help with are medical problems.
If someone tells you, he can cure cancer or something big like this with hypnosis alone, be very careful and cautious.
And whatever you do, never quit a medical procedure because you want to switch to hypnotherapy alone.
If you don't like your medical procedure, get another doctor to look at you.
Hypnosis can assist complementary to medical problems, but it shouldn't replace medical procedures.
It can lend a hand with pain management. Hypnotical Anesthesia has been around for thousands of years. It can also help to give you a better outlook on your future, boost your mood, and stimulate your immune system by reducing stress. But all those things should be complementary.

Can Hypnosis help with Stage fright

The biggest question for this book is, can hypnosis help with stage fright? Ab-so-lutely.

Fears, phobias, and worries are some of the easiest to get rid of mental issues. Often in one session, like my spider phobia.

Depending on your level of fear and your trust in your hypnotist and the process, maybe up to three sessions.

If it is still there at the same level after three sessions, there is probably something else going on. Still, you should be able to see positive results regardless.

What hypnosis can also do, is, find out why you have this problem, and what underlying beliefs you have that hinder you from getting on stage and having fun doing so.

Are you sabotaging yourself somehow?

This is not a necessity to implore but if you want to know, it is a good start to unravel your problem. For some clients this is a light bulb moment and that changes a lot.

Hypnosis can also boost your confidence, so that you know what you are worth. Boosting confidence is not hard. And if you do not want a full hypnotherapy session on it, I put something in the Resource Section for you.

If you want to know if hypnosis is for your problem or when you still have questions about the procedure, find a hypnotherapist you like and get a short first call. They are mostly free.

What you are not getting in this free call, is a free session. Please don't insult professionals by begging for free sessions. You wouldn't go to a doctor or a car mechanic and ask them to do their job for free.

We may have not gone to medical school, but our training normally isn't cheap either. And most of us continue learning throughout our life because this field is so broad and new knowledge is coming up all the time.

About that little bonus

A while ago I promised you some kind of bonus for reading through the book. Here it comes.
I am sorry to say, that it only applies to men. If you are a woman and have some idea how I could use this for women, please contact me. I would be thankful for any idea.

Your body and mind are a wonder. Your body can recreate everything it has encountered before.
This is sometimes used with patients who got morphine as a pain medication while in hospital.
Of course, morphine is highly addictive, and you shouldn't take it any longer than absolutely necessary.
The funny thing is, once you have gotten it, your body can remember and create it again without the side effects. This linkage is used in pain management through hypnosis.
Therefor, we can use this effect of creating anything our body once felt and move it around to where we want it.

By this time, you are very aware of and familiar with stage fright and freezing.

How about we move your freezing around to a body part that should stand a little longer and numb it a bit so that it doesn't come too fast?

It is doable. Ask your hypnotist if he/she is willing to anchor this effect for you, so you can use it if needed. Not everyone knows how to do this or is comfortable with this topic, so ask before in your free call.
A little warning, it only gives you a few seconds more, depending on your visualization and anchoring. Too long would create pain. But I think it is worth a try. Have fun with it.

Where to go

You can find hypnotherapists or hypnotists locally in your community. Nowadays many professionals, like me, are using online sessions worldwide. Just find us on the internet. Some schools, like Marisa Peer's RTT school also have lists with names of their students and their information.
If you want to look me up, go to www.andreastrunz.com. If you have a different problem, I may not be the specialist you seek but we can talk about that.

Online sessions work great. You don't have to travel to see someone. A computer with a microphone and headphones is enough. I prefer my clients to wear headsets with microphones because I think that the sound is better and there are fewer outside disturbances but that is up to you.
Mobiles work not so well from the hypnotist's point of view because we can't really see you and so we can't always monitor your body indicators.
Find someone who conducts a session either in your mother tongue or in a language you are very familiar with.

And you should be able to talk in this other language because your hypnotist should be asking you lots of questions.

Similarly make sure your hypnotist has some kind of credibility, like a license, and is a member of a professional body like the IAPCP.

What kind of Hypnosis do you recommend

There are different schools out there, therefore there are different ways of how to conduct a session. In the end, they are all similar of course but the used techniques differ a little and everyone tweaks them a little to their liking.
Mostly it is not the techniques, even though some are better than others, but your motivation and the hypnotist himself/herself that gets you results. Put in a little research as to what you want. I would start on YouTube with the big names and then find a student of theirs.

My teacher often used the analogy of a garden to describe what she was doing.
Most hypnotists plant new seeds in your garden. Some even water them afterward.
Others, like RTT Therapists take out all the old weeds before they plant new seeds and then water them, so that the weeds don't strangle the new, still delicate plants.
All three methods are valuable. Some are a little better but that is often personal preference or marketing. And I may be a little biased here as is every hypnotist out there.

If you don't have a preference for a certain method, find someone you are comfortable with and you can trust.

You don't need to click in all matters, but you should at least respect your hypnotist. Liking the hypnotist's voice also helps, otherwise you will have a hard time going into a deep relaxation.

Should you have money issues, try finding a hypnotist in another country, where they are charging less. Some hypnotists even have payment plans.

How fast do I see results

This is a good question. From the meta-study I quoted earlier, many issues are gone after six hours of hypnosis. This should be around 2-3 sessions, depending on the length of a session. Mine are between two to three hours, depending on what is coming up.
There should be a month between sessions because your brain needs time to change and build new roads. Sessions can be in a shorter interval, like before giving birth for example, but one month is quite normal.

Otherwise, it all depends on you.
It is subject to your problem, fears and phobias for example are relatively easy to overcome. Other issues, like eating disorders, definitely need more time. And a specialist.

Your motivation for getting rid of something is a huge part of your success.
If you really want it and are prepared to do the work, meaning talking to your hypnotist, trusting the way he/she works even if it goes against your critical thinking, and doing your homework – I was a teacher. I give you homework – then your chances are good that you will be free of your problem soon.

How your brain works is also important and there is nothing we can do about it.
Some people have a light bulb moment and change in an instant.
My teacher told us a story about a man who came to her because of his alcoholism. He wanted to change, he was fed up and he had a huge respect for her as a hypnotherapist. So, he went into a trance even before my teacher could speak him into it and after a short session, he woke up, thanked her because he felt better, and hadn't had a single drink since. Those are ideal clients. But they are sadly not common.

My clients always say that they feel different after a session. Lighter and more relaxed but issue-related changes arrive mostly gradually step by step. You will see a change here and there and then suddenly something else in your life is different, too. So, the changes can bleed out into other areas as well. You can kill two birds with one stone.
Some people only change in hindsight. You ask them for example, when they had their last stress-related migraine and they say something like ahhh, now that you are asking, I can't really remember.

My spider phobia was like that. I was terrified of spiders my whole life.

One of my colleagues gave me a training session on it, meaning the session wasn't even complete, so I had no reason to think that it would work at all. I just forgot about it.
I didn't feel any change for three months because I hadn't encountered a spider until I suddenly saw a huge spider sitting on our garage wall.
Instead of running away screaming, with a gagging reflex as I would before, I went to it, had a good look at it and starting to pity the thing because winter was coming. Only then did I stop thinking and I realized that I wasn't afraid anymore.

Your expectation is key again.
A story Paul McKenna likes to tell is about a client who had sleeping problems, he couldn't sleep and would lay awake for hours. After one session they didn't see each other for a while. Meeting again by chance the client told my teacher that it hadn't worked.
Being confused, Paul McKenna asked, was there no change at all? Nothing? How often can you sleep through the night? The answer was only 85% of the time.
Well, for me from zero to 85% sleep is a big success but maybe you see it differently.
By the way, people don't sleep through the night. Everyone wakes up around four times within 7-8 hours of sleep but goes back to sleep immediately and forgets about it.

"The Show must go on"

– Freddie Mercury, Queen

Chapter 9

About how to go on from here

We are coming to the end of this book. In your hands are the most effective techniques against stage fright up to date. I hope this is the manual you have been waiting for all your life. You can finally lay your gremlin to rest now. You do deserve a better life and having fun on stage. Rock your life.

If you want to learn more about the things I told you in this book, go to the Resources Section. Next to the materials I used to write this book. I also put in further materials, that could be of interest to you.

One is Paul McKenna's book, Instant Confidence. As it is a little difficult to get by, there is a free YouTube link to the trance that comes with the book.
Listen to it for at least 21 days in a row, best before you fall asleep or shortly after you have woken up.

Otherwise, I can recommend all works of Paul McKenna and Marisa Peer. See what speaks to you. Some prefer the one over the other. They have many things on YouTube for free.
And no, I don't get anything for promoting this stuff. I do it because I think it will help you live a better life without suffering. It rocked my world, let it rock yours.

If you are looking for a hypnotherapist or an RTT therapist, you are welcome to look me up at www.andreastrunz.com or find someone that suits your needs better.
It is okay to not like someone and for a good hypnotherapy relationship a kind of mutual attraction is important otherwise you don't have to start to begin with. This means it could happen, that your hypnotist decides not to work with you, too because you rub him the wrong way or he/she is not comfortable with your issue. It has nothing to do with you as a human being. It has more to do with giving you a better chance for a good and fast change.

If you have some time, I would be delighted, if you would write a comment on Amazon. Those reviews are important for authors to be more visible and help new readers decide if it is for them. Thank you in advance. I really appreciate your time. If you have any suggestions for further topics, write them in your comments. It may not be my next book, but I am up for ideas.

If you want to know more, follow me on Amazon, as I will publish more books in this series on different topics. Have a look at my website now and again, as I plan to expand on it as far as time allows. If you have forgotten it already, I can be found at www.andreastrunz.com

So far so good. One more tiny chapter to go.

> "Plaudite, amici, comedia finita est.
> (Applaud, my friends, the comedy is over.)
> [*Said on his deathbed*]" — Ludwig van Beethoven

Chapter 10

About Final Words and such

Thank you again for reading this book. My wish in writing it was and still is, to help as many people as I can to get rid of stage fright, which is total unnecessary suffering.
I sincerely hope it helped you overcome your problem, if not, please go back to Havening® and do it because there is no way that it didn't work.

And thank you from the bottom of my heart for buying this book. Writing a book needs time, effort, and financial resources and it takes energy away from earning money otherwise.

Every bought book brings me one step closer to writing a bestseller and let's be honest, as we are all human, including me, a bestseller would be a dream come true for every author.

So, to all my readers out there, I salute you and a heartfelt thank you. You rock! And maybe I will be in the audience next time you are on stage cheering you up and cheering for you.

Andrea Strunz

Resource Section

National Library of Medicine:
The biology of fear, PhD Thierry Steimer
https://www.ncbi.nlm.nih.gov/pmc/articles/
PMC3181681/

Encyclopedia:
https://www.encyclopedia.com/psychology/
encyclopedias-almanacs-transcripts-and-maps/fear-
conditioning-freezing

The Conversation:
https://theconversation.com/paralysed-with-fear-why-
do-we-freeze-when-frightened-60543

Modern Therapy Online:
https://moderntherapy.online/blog-2/2020/6/7/frozen-in-
fear-understanding-the-freeze-response-within-anxiety

Wikipedia:
https://en.wikipedia.org/wiki/Stage_fright

Wikipedia:
https://en.wikipedia.org/wiki/Fight-or-flight_response

Hello Music Theory:
https://hellomusictheory.com/learn/famous-musicians-
with-stage-fright/

Yoga easy (in German):
https://www.yogaeasy.de/artikel/sieben-auf-einen-
streich#manipura

Havening®:
https://havening.org/index.php

Paul McKenna shows Havening®:
https://www.youtube.com/watch?v=69e11xGNJUg

Choosing therapy:
https://www.choosingtherapy.com/stage-fright/

Basketball Study:
https://www.breakthroughbasketball.com/mental/
visualization.html

History of Hypnosis
https://hypno-institut.com/geschichte-der-hypnose/

Comparing hypnosis and psychotherapy
Alfred A. Barrios, Ph.D., in Psychotherapy Magazine,
v7n1, and in Theory, Research, and Practice, Spring
1970

IAPCP: International Alliance of Professional
Complementary Practitioners
https://www.iapcp.org/

Further Materials

Paul McKenna, Instant Confidence, 2006

Paul McKenna – Confidence Audio:
https://www.youtube.com/watch?v=9nTcDbRnyCo

Marisa Peer, Ultimate Confidence, 2005

About the Author

Andrea Strunz started her professional life as a social worker, changing to teaching German as a foreign language for adults, including health care personnel and doctors, also published many books in this area, one of them being translated into approximately 20 languages and counting.

Around Covid she began training, first as an RTT therapist (Rapid transformational therapy) and then as a hypnotherapist with a good pinch of NLP (Neuro-Linguistic Programming). She had the honor of training under some of the most famous hypnotherapists of her time, leading with Marisa Peer, Paul McKenna, and Richard Bandler among others.

She specializes in working with artists, like musicians, actors, writers, and others because she knows her way around there. In her private life she had been on stage as a semiprofessional swordfighter, sadly, but good for her students and clients, never finished her training to become a stage director. She tries following her passion for Hard Rock and Heavy Metal as much as her time permits.

Andrea can be found at www.andreastrunz.com

Glossary

Carl Gustav Jung (1875-1961):
Swiss psychiatrist and psychoanalyst who founded analytical psychology, friends with Sigmund Freud, seen as one of the most influential psychologists in history.

Event Havening ®:
a type of Havening® that concentrates on one past event

Gymnasium:
the highest form of secondary education; aims to prepare students for continued university education.

Haiku:
Japanese lyric verse form having three unrhymed lines of five, seven, and five syllables, traditionally invoking an aspect of nature or the seasons.

Havening®:
a relatively new technique using sensory input like touch, sound, and sight to change thoughts, moods, and behaviors

Hypnosis:
Trance, Deep Relaxation, natural state of mind that is used to focus attention.

Hypnotherapist:
A person who uses hypnosis to help other people with mental issues; often a hypnotist and hypnotherapist is interchangeable, depending on the country there can be a difference in methods and educational background.

Hypnotherapy:
a type of mind–body intervention in which hypnosis is used to create a state of focused attention and increased suggestibility in the treatment of a medical or psychological disorder or concern

Hypnotist:
Person who uses hypnosis to help other people with mental issues; often hypnotist and hypnotherapist is interchangeable, depending on the country there can be a difference in methods and educational background

Marisa Peer:
British therapist, best-selling author, transformational leader, and creator of the 'I Am Enough' movement, award-winning founder of Rapid Transformational Therapy (RTT®)

Never change a running system:
German phrase used in German with English words for "if it ain't broke, don't fix it"

NLP:
Neuro-linguistic programming

Paul McKenna, Dr.:
British hypnotist, behavioral scientist, television and radio broadcaster, and author of bestselling self-help books, McKenna specializes in working with PTSD, severe trauma, pain control, and emotional overwhelm.
Involved in a research study conducted by Professor Neil Greenberg of The Royal College of Psychiatrists Lead for Military and Veterans' Health

Psycho-sensory:
a technique: meaning it uses sensory input like touch, sound, and sight to change your thoughts, moods, and behaviors.

PTSD:
Post-traumatic stress disorder (PTSD), is a mental and behavioral disorder that develops from experiencing a traumatic event, such as sexual assault, warfare, traffic collisions, child abuse, domestic violence, or other threats to a person's life or well-being.

Richard Bandler, Dr.:
Co-founder of NLP together with John Grinder

Ronald A. Ruden, Dr.:
Creator of The Havening® Techniques

RTT®:
Rapid Transformational Therapy; a form of therapy founded by Marisa Peer, the roots of RTT® are drawn from within areas of traditional psychotherapy such as gestalt, solution-focused and cognitive behavioral therapy, hypnotherapy, and mindfulness

Sigmund Freud (1856-1936):
Austrian neurologist and the founder of psychoanalysis

Stage Combat Director:
also, Theater Fight Director; responsible for planning, choreographing, and overseeing staged combat (fights) in a film, play, or other performance, making the fight as realistic as possible and safe for the actors

Stage fright:
A state of nervousness about performing some action in front of a group of people, on or off of a stage; nerves; uncertainty; a lack of self-assurance before an audience.

Self-Help Books published by Andrea Strunz

Series:
A Little Book of Horrors and How to Deal with Them

Book 1: Getting Rid of Heartache

Book 2: Getting Rid of Stage Fright

more to come

SOON TO COME

Andrea Strunz

Series:
A Little Book of Horrors and How to Deal with
Them

Book 3